Full Circle

Full Circle

Fifteen Ways to Grow Lifelong UUs

Kate Tweedie Erslev

UNITARIAN UNIVERSALIST ASSOCIATION
BOSTON

Dedicated to my mother, Sally Bersey Tweedie, my role model, who taught UU Sunday School for sixteen years.
—Kate Tweedie Erslev

Copyright © 2004 by the Unitarian Universalist Association, 25 Beacon Street, Boston, MA 02108-2800. All rights reserved.

Printed in Canada.

ISBN 1-55896-475-4

10 9 8 7 6 5 4 3 2 1
08 07 06 05 04

Excerpt from "Little Gidding" in *Four Quartets*, copyright 1942 by T. S. Eliot and renewed 1970 by Esme Valerie Eliot, reprinted by permission of Harcourt, Inc.

We shall not cease from exploration
And the end of all our exploring
Will be to arrive where we started
And know the place for the first time.
—from T. S. Eliot, "Little Gidding"

Contents

Foreword ix

Introduction xiii

1. Embrace Our UU Identity 1

2. Recognize Religious Education as an
   Important Portal to Institutional Involvement 11

3. Share the Value of Attending Regularly, at Least
   Three Times a Month 17

4. Ritualize Holiday Events and Celebratory Activities 20

5. Prepare All for the Negative Side of Community 27

6. Provide Background for Teachers in
   Every Weekly Session Plan 34

7. Provide Parent Handouts in Every Session Plan 37

8. Offer Opportunities for All Ages to Live Out UU Values 40

9. Offer Engaging Church School for Kindergarten
through Sixth Grade 45

10. Take Every Opportunity for Ministers and
Lay Leaders to Mentor Children and Teens 51

11. Sweep Teens into Immersion Experiences 56

12. Bolster and Protect Youth Groups 62

13. Connect with Our Young Adults 68

14. Sing Together 76

15. Celebrate Founders, Lifers and Heritage 79

Conclusion 85

The Survey 88

Resources 95

Foreword

WHEN CHRISTIAN EDUCATOR John H. Westerhoff challenged churches in the last century with the question, "Will our children have faith?," he was responding to widespread concern at that time that outdated methodologies and traditions were making religious education irrelevant to the contemporary issues youth faced.

The question posed to twenty-first century religious professionals at a recent UU conference was, "Will our faith have children?" At issue was the current mass exodus of young people from their religion of origin. We know that the majority of Unitarian Universalists were raised outside our faith, and also that the majority of people raised UU do not remain active in our movement. We are not alone in this pattern of exodus, which all mainstream faiths experience to some extent, but that fact is no consolation to those of us who want to ensure that we offer a religious home so relevant, meaningful, and sustaining that our children will choose to remain Unitarian Universalists throughout their lives.

While many religious leaders have asked, "Why do they leave?, " religious educator Kate Erslev has asked, instead, "Why did you *stay?*" A Unitarian Universalist lifer herself, Erslev has surveyed and interviewed eighty-two men and women ranging in age from twenty-five to eighty-seven who were raised as Unitarian Universalists, either from birth or from early school-age. The results—some expected, some surprising—are presented here as fifteen ways to grow (and keep) Unitarian Universalists.

This engaging book is not merely interesting; it is useful. A congregation can use this as a resource for their own reflection and action in the following ways:

- *Leadership.* The professional staff can read this resource and discuss its implications for the professional and lay ministry of the congregation. *What are best practices for faith development?*
- *Evaluation.* The congregational board, religious education committee, and membership committees can use this resource as a basis for evaluating the congregation's ability to nurture a sense of belonging and a commitment to our faith. *Is there something we could do better?*
- *Experience.* The congregation can invite its members who are lifelong UUs to share their experiences, reflections, and sug-

gestions through a focus group, interview, fish bowl, or worship service. *What can we learn from them?*

- *Growth.* Any congregational group focusing on growth can use this resource to develop growth strategies, because what keeps birthright UUs in the fold attracts and keeps seekers, too. *What are the connections between maintaining congregations and growing them?*

In *Fashion Me a People*, religious educator Maria Harris suggests that the entire course of a church's life is its curriculum—that everything a church says, does, and does not do "teaches" what that religious community is all about. *Full Circle* demonstrates that every person and every activity in the congregation can contribute to individual faith development and congregational growth and vitality. I hope this book will likewise serve as a catalyst for spirited conversation, reflection, and action in our congregations as they build the beloved community.

Judith Frediani
Director, Lifespan Faith Development
Unitarian Universalist Association

Introduction

ONE NIGHT DURING General Assembly in 1997, I asked my companions around the dinner table how many had grown up Unitarian Universalist. Out of ten people, eight responded that they had grown up in the faith. As we told our stories, we experienced the friendly telepathy that comes from common experiences. The group sounded like an old married couple that finishes sentences for each other. Why so many children who grow up Unitarian Universalist eventually leave the faith is a compelling question, but the mutual understanding that I felt that night inspired me to look at the issue in another way: What causes a person to make a lifelong commitment to Unitarian Universalism? By investigating the common threads among people who remain UUs, we may be able to capitalize on those elements of our faith that keep people coming back.

In 1998, I received a grant from the Unitarian Sunday School Society to gather together the stories of lifelong UUs through a process that included an informal survey and interviews. People sent me written descriptions of their experiences, some of which had been previously published. I encouraged all participants to tell me about both negative and positive reactions to Unitarian Universalism in their lives. Respondents shared engaging, poignant, and often funny stories. Some are national leaders, such as former Unitarian Universalist Association president William Schulz and former religious education director Eugene Navias. Some are members of families that have been Unitarian or Universalist for several generations. All of the stories are worth listening to, and a sense of Unitarian Universalism's greatest strengths emerges from this collective memory. Each chapter that follows discusses one of these common threads and offers testimonials to the important place that our faith holds in individual lives.

For the purpose of this discussion, I have defined "lifelong UU" as someone who was born and/or raised Unitarian, Universalist, or Unitarian Universalist. My focus on those who have grown up in our faith is in no way intended to set them above those who have come into our faith later in life. Newcomers are also important for their understanding of other faiths and their perspective on what is inviting about Unitarian Universalism. We need the stories of their courage of conviction as they searched for a religious home. And those who come to us without any faith background are important as well. They bring their stories of the compelling search for transcendence and spirituality, the need for a faith community, and their joy in finding one such as ours. All Unitarian Universalists can tell us about who we are. All of these stories make up our Unitarian Universalist community.

Kate Tweedie Erslev
May 2004

1

Embrace Our UU Identity

IN A DISCUSSION conducted on an e-mail listserv for Unitarian Universalist religious educators, Riley McLaughlin, Director of Religious Education in San Francisco, writes,

> Is joining a UU congregation equivalent to "being a Unitarian Universalist?" I know many Jews who are not members of synagogues, Catholics who are not members of churches, and so forth. Indeed, some of the most dedicated and active UUs I know are not members of a congregation.... So when we raise children to be UUs, are we raising them specifically to join a UU congregation, or to be sustained by UU values in their lifelong effort to be wonderful people?

Riley's comments capture the dilemma that many UUs confront. At a very basic level, we often cannot clearly articulate whether we want to create "good UUs" or "wonderful people." This is the largest stumbling block we face in creating a lifelong commitment to our faith. In that same e-mail dialogue, the Reverend Francis Manly outlines what can be missed if we don't embrace our UU identity:

> It seems to me that if the majority of our kids continue to grow up to be "small-u" UUs (but join Episcopalian or Presbyterian churches because that's what their spouses are, or join no church at all) then we have not entirely failed, but we have failed in something important. That is, we have not helped them to understand and to feel that Unitarian Universalism is indeed a real faith tradition in its own right rather than just a place to learn about religion.

Manly's conclusion contrasts sharply with the comments of many lifelong UUs, who take their faith as a given. When asked what might cause them to leave, they often shrugged their shoulders and paused. "I could never be anything else," responds the Reverend Emily Morse Palmer. Others, including the Reverend Margaret K. Gooding, echo this sentiment. In a 1974 religious education essay, she writes,

> The records of the township of Langdon, New Hampshire, show that in 1801 one William King purchased a pew in the

Universalist meeting house for the sum of $40.00. Thus began a family religious heritage ... that has led to my arrival in our church to serve as religious education director.... I have grown up Universalist and have never wanted to be anything else. My religious ideas have changed as Universalism has changed but it has been a gradual and not a dramatic change.

It is time we start embracing a Unitarian Universalist identity. Our goal should be a lifelong commitment to the UU faith and a devotion to humankind imparted through strong UU religious education. We need not fear the traditional understanding of "church school," as Gabriel Moran describes it in his book *Religious Body*— "officials of a church indoctrinating children to obey an official church." Moran's definition helps us see how our Catholic sisters and brothers and members of other traditional faiths sometimes feel—that there is some fundamental contradiction between theory and practice, between sprituality and worldliness that forces them to choose between being good adherents to their faith or good world citizens. Unitarian Universalist religious education should insist that we do not have to make such a choice.

Neglecting to foster a UU identity is similar to leaving the meaning of the Bible to the Fundamentalists. It is time to clarify who we are. When it comes to religious education, this means creating lifelong learners, responsible decision makers, and agents of transformation in the world who recognize the power of being in UU community. *We need to embrace our identity and make our expectations explicit.*

In her book *Educating in Faith*, Mary Boys identifies historical factors that have influenced the dilemma some of us experience in embracing a UU identity. She describes the religious education movement in liberal Protestantism, including the brand of Unitarianism and Universalism practiced in the late nineteenth century, that sought to instill "a devotion to humankind" and saw education as a means of fostering the "reconstruction of society." The understanding of "religious education" promulgated in this movement included a generalized hope for creating good people.

UU religious education is one of the classic expressions of the kind of progressive religious education that Boys describes. She makes special note of Sophia Lyons Fahs, a former editor of children's materials for the American Unitarian Association, as "the religious educator who most brilliantly embodied 'creative personal and social experience' for the young." Thus our roots—and our dilemmas—are derived from progressive educational theory along with a history of liberal theology.

Mainstream Christianity pulled away from the ideals of progressive liberalism in the wake of the World Wars and the Great Depression. These cataclysmic events severely challenged the idealized vision of progress towards a higher good, of the evolution of society toward enlightenment. Unitarian Universalist Principles, on the other hand, continue to reflect this liberal theological outlook and the educational theories upon which it is based. Ours is one of the few faiths that remains committed to this idealism.

By reflecting on our history we come to understand our identity and our roots, and we can then embrace them and learn from them. Embracing a UU identity means that we start explicitly teaching those elements that we all too often simply assume. My colleague, the Reverend W. Roy Jones Jr., first introduced these issues to me in a sermon entitled, "Our Hidden Commitments." Jones speaks about the hidden assumptions that underlie our faith. If we brought these to the fore, our religious education programs would teach about beliefs that we hold dear:

- There is the possibility of good in the universe.
- The ultimate religious act is choosing.
- We make choices with intelligent love.
- We learn best when in community.

These statements are, of course, not scientifically verifiable. Science cannot tell us whether obedience or choice is always preferable. But as a matter of faith, we believe that choice—based on all that we know, and always allowing for the possibility of change as we learn more—is the ultimate religious act.

Similarly, many in UU congregations believe that revelation is not best sought alone on a mountaintop. While some of us do find sources of inspiration in that way, we believe that a community is a crucible that helps us to share our religious ideas and questions and mature religiously.

The Reverend Rebecca Parker, president of the Starr King School for the Ministry, further reveals our implicit theology in a lecture entitled "The Theology of Religious Education," given at the Liberal Religious Educators' Conference in Fall 2002. Her presentation provides a powerful metaphor for our UU identity. She invites us to view our Unitarian Universalist faith as a house situated in a neighborhood of other houses that represent other faiths. She suggests that classical theological terms can describe the form of each house. The foundation is *theology* (the basis of our humanness); the windows, *missiology* (our relation to our neighbors);the doors and threshold, *eschatology* (the final endpoint of our faith); the roof, *soteriology* (our protection and salvation); and the environment immediately outside our house, *pneumatology* (the web of life that surrounds us). Parker uses these metaphors to identify the characteristics of our faith in words that allow us to draw parallels with other faiths. By drawing distinctions among the particular elements that comprise each "faith house," we can visualize a UU identity that we can teach, avoiding the common misunderstanding that Unitarian Universalism is a faith in which people simply believe anything they want to believe.

To date, UU identity has largely been taught implicitly. Some of us have learned about our individual faith through introspection; others have connected with it through family identification. Betsy Robinson describes the sometimes circuitous path taken by lifelong

UUs as they try to discern their own theology:

> I remember that in high school I decided that I had to figure out what I believed. I went through a long process and a frustrating one. I realized that kids from traditional churches didn't have to go through this process—I was jealous. But I never considered converting. I guess I came up with some beliefs at that time that have periodically been revised. I could never not be a UU.

Our theology—the foundation of our house, according to Parker's metaphor—is based upon our belief that we have the power to choose. We can use our reason, our senses, and our conscience to aid us in making choices. As Robinson's story shows, lifers often come to this realization on their own, but for many UUs the search for their theological house can be a hit-or-miss effort. Consider the twin experiences of Dan Boyce and his wife:

> I grew up UU. My wife grew up Methodist. When we first started dating, we were both in the University of Michigan School of Music Choir. We were on a bus going to a performance and passed the Ann Arbor UU Church. Not yet knowing my religious affiliation, but having had a sorority sister who was UU, she said, "You know—that's a religion that makes sense to me." Upon declaring my affiliation, we had a good laugh—she might just have easily been sticking

her foot in her mouth. The rest is history—we were married at the Ann Arbor UU Church a year and a half later.

Robin Stitzel's description of a friend's experience dramatically illustrates what can happen when a precise explication of UU beliefs is not part of growing up UU:

> My best friend, Alison, and I were both raised in the same [UU] church. Her grandparents and mine all joined in 1935. Their daughters grew up in the church and raised their families there too. She no longer belongs to this church—having returned several times and tried to "come home," she has finally concluded that it is no longer her church. She once remarked that she was raised as a "nothing," not a UU; she didn't feel that her UU years had given her anything.
>
> I feel quite differently. My feelings for the church are tangled up with family memories and I feel that I got the base of my ethical and moral outlook from my UU years. I'm sure that because we moved away when I was twelve, and I never felt that anywhere was home except Fort Collins, that the church was part of my feelings of security and home. I cannot help but feel the presence of my grandparents when I'm in church. This was such a big part of their lives and my continuity in it sustains me.

Here's another dramatic example, relating how Priscilla Greene

Osgood had to discover the implicit message of our faith on her own as a UU teen:

> At thirteen my mother told me it was time to join the church. Me: "Why?" She: "Because your brother and sister did at that age." Me: "No thanks." And then I went to other churches with various friends. One friend was trying to "save" me—I was accustomed to this and generally just let it roll off my back. However, once I stayed overnight at her house and attended her Baptist Church in a blue-collar area of Philadelphia. When she introduced me to her minister as "Priscilla Greene," he gave me a big warm smile and said, "Well, as long as you're not black!" I was startled, but thought I had misunderstood him—after all, this was a minister. Then, in the Sunday school class, the teacher was talking about how tough it was to be a missionary in Africa—she said, "Can you imagine teaching all those black faces!" Now I was really uncomfortable! I assumed all churches taught that we are created equal, and I had bought it hook, line, and sinker, so the idea of finding racial prejudice being embraced *within a church* was totally paradoxical to me. During the church service that followed, the minister preached hell-fire and damnation with great energy. Feeling physically sick, I left the church and waited outside for my friend. Visiting other churches was not as dramatic as this but in the long

run I guess I had set up my own "Church Across the Street."
By finding what I didn't and couldn't believe, I learned the
substance of my religion.

We seem to teach our faith implicitly. In the fifties, sixties, and
seventies we made it clear what we "weren't," but we did not stake
a claim as to what we were. We left our children to discover our
implicit beliefs by themselves. Today, we make use of our Principles
and Sources to guide religious education curricula and to inform
our actions. But we still are not articulating our UU identity very
well. It is time to put aside our reluctance to describe ourselves as a
faith with a concrete identity and to begin to describe the "house"
that we live in.

2

Recognize Religious Education as an Important Portal to Institutional Involvement

MANY NEW FAMILIES come to Unitarian Universalist churches looking for a religious community in which to raise their children. Part of their motive for joining, as well as their first experiences in the UU community, naturally revolve around religious education. Many lifelong UUs enjoyed their first leadership experiences in the context of religious education. Several lifers included in the survey were asked to teach in their teen years and included these experiences as positive highlights. They felt empowered and honored and took their responsibility seriously. For Jane Clayton, these adolescent experiences provided the foundation for a lifetime commitment to Unitarian Universalism:

I started teaching in the religious education program while I was in my teens, after participating in the program as a child. I taught three-year-olds and followed them year by year until they were seven. At this point I moved away from Ottawa. I had many years of early exposure to a UU way of looking at the world. This has sustained me throughout my life.

Some in the UU ministry, like the Reverend Elizabeth M. Strong, also discovered the seeds of their vocation through early educational leadership experiences:

> I taught religious education when I was in the eighth grade using books like *Beginnings*, *Jesus the Carpenter's Son*, *Moses*, and *Joseph and the Twelve Brothers*. I went to state Universalist convention meetings. My father was president and held every other office for the convention.

In order to promote a lifelong commitment to Unitarian Universalism, we should acknowledge that the core stewardship of the congregation and denomination often begins with teaching religious education. We should create a path with identifiable stepping stones, starting with religious education, that leads to opportunities for rich rewards and lifelong commitment.

We can ask lifelong UUs to share their wealth of knowledge about religious education "from the inside" and invite them to lead classes. From there we can lead them into stewardship roles in all facets of church governance and community in order to satisfy the need for depth and commitment that lifers seek.

Lifelong UUs explain that when they were in high school, they were most comfortable at first serving in religious education roles, having grown up in church school themselves. Lifers regale us with memories of leadership from childhood on—they lit candles, played parts in celebrations, and helped in congregational events. Twelve respondents mention holding an office in their congregation's youth group.

Teaching religious education is also the most commonly noted leadership opportunity mentioned among lifers' memories of their young adult years (twenty-two to thirty years old). Once they become interested in being involved again, young adult lifers seem to gravitate to teaching. Of those who responded to the survey, ten note that participating in religious education provided an opportunity for leadership in their twenties, while only four served on the Board of Trustees and a mere two were involved with the congregation on a professional level during this period in their lives.

Between the ages of thirty-one and fifty, lifers' involvement tended to blossom into all facets of institutional life. More survey respondents participated in their congregations during this stage in their lives as board members, in canvassing and finance, and in the ministry. They also mention many other facets of congregational life, such as service on personnel, membership, nominating, bylaw, social action, and endowment committees, as well as experiences establishing a new fellowship, serving on a ministerial search committee, or participating in church auction, choir, yoga, and long range planning. Reverend Albert C. Niles describes his UU leadership experiences in more than ninety years of life: "As a liberal minister serving at all levels for over sixty years now, I've probably forgotten more leadership roles than I could remember."

At the same time, involvement in religious education continues to offer the most opportunities to UUs in this age group, with eight serving as teachers, four as directors of religious education, and five as religious education chairs. In our recruiting of teachers we should actively seek out those who have grown up in UU religious education programs, both in high school and as young adults, as their experience helps make them excellent teachers. Encourage religious education teachers to serve on religious education committees or Sunday service committees. Send your incoming religious education chairperson to leadership school or a continuing education workshop. You can expect and encourage religious education leadership to attend district conferences or General Assembly and provide financial support.

We need to actively question whether we are providing the encouragement and opportunities needed to capitalize on our members' leadership experiences in religious education. For example, do you recruit the outgoing religious education chair to join the Board of Trustees? Do you tell your high school youth and young adults about opportunities for professional leadership in the denomination? Then as our lifers age we can offer opportunities for wider and wider denominational involvement. One lifelong UU in her seventies, Evelyn Frain of Ontario, Canada, wrote of her delight in international UU involvement:

> A tremendously positive experience was attending the European Unitarian Retreat in 1996, first a visit to Oxford, England, where the Unitarian ministers are trained at Manchester College, then the retreat itself at Canterbury, England. All European Unitarians were represented: Czech, Hungarian, Danish, Dutch, German, French, and many British. The universality of Unitarianism should be more widely known and eulogized. It is not just a North American phenomenon.

By identifying and providing channels for early leaders to grow, we nurture their appetite for increased, lifelong commitment. "UU Young Adults may have just finished four or fourteen years of Unitarian Universalist religious education. They don't want it to suddenly end, or to go to waste," says Sharon Hwang Colligan in *Children of a Different Tribe*. Rather than letting these sensibilities languish, we need to steer our beginning leaders toward feeling the power of communal social witness at General Assembly and having their hearts swell with pride at the banner parade. We want our members to feel the power of crafting worship experiences and sharing deeply at Evensong circles. In short, we want to use their religious education experiences as a springboard to making a lifelong commitment to stewardship of a Unitarian Universalist congregation.

3

Share the Value of Attending Regularly, at Least Three Times a Month

IN EDUCATING FAMILIES that are new to the church on how to be involved in a religious community, it is important to stress the benefits of attending services regularly. Lifers reveal a common thread of regular attendance over the years in their survey responses. Average individual attendance was four times per month during the childhood years. For lifers like Priscilla Osgood, the routines established early in life proved important in sustaining her own lifelong commitment:

> I'm a fourth-generation Universalist—passed down through the women. My grandmother took her two daughters to the Universalist Church in Cooperstown, New York, while my

grandfather took the two boys to the Presbyterian Church. My parents, especially my mother, were very involved with the Universalist Church of the Restoration in Philadelphia. I attended because it was expected of me.

Likewise, Dorothy Brown explains the significance of a regular routine in establishing these lifelong habits:

I'm sure I was there every Sunday but I can't remember those early years. My only memory is going with my father (I would have been five or six) to the church on the wagon filled with wood and coal, driven by our horses, to put wood and coal in the basement bin. He would remove a basement window, dump our wagon, and start the old furnace so the church would be warm before services.

In order to participate in the vision, meaning, and values of the church, children and parents need to come often enough to be a part of the community. In sharing the importance of regular atten-dance, we should encourage families in a balanced, non-threatening way to set a goal of attending three or four times per month. We can expect and encourage this regularity while children are young; once the children enter the teen years, expectations for regular Sunday school attendance may need to shift to regular involvement in youth group activities. Respondents' attendance during their teen years averaged between 3.3 and 3.8 days per month. The Reverend

Eugene Navias explains that in his case, additional activities were essential to keeping him involved:

> I went to Sunday school since our family went to church faithfully. Part of what motivated me was an attendance reward in the form of little metal bars. If you were a really good little attender you got a bar each year and it was attached to the bar above, and eventually, since I had a decade of perfect attendance, I had bars jangling all the way down my little chest to my belly button.
>
> Sunday school was fine, but it paled in the upper elementary years, and if it hadn't been for the junior high youth group, and skating parties on Collins Pond, and hot chocolate . . . I don't think I ever would have made it.

New families may not understand some of the assumptions implicit in being involved in a faith community and people who grow up in unchurched families often wonder what the rules are. It helps to have explicit recommendations about such issues as attendance and pledging in order to make newcomers feel more comfortable. Joining a UU congregation is not the same as joining the Sierra Club or the Brownies. We offer support for a life-enriching, lifelong journey that involves the whole family through the calamities and joys of life. We need to welcome and encourage our members to partake of the community at least three times a month in order to reap the full benefits of religious community.

4

Ritualize Holiday Events and Celebratory Activities

I HAVE A VIVID MEMORY of sitting with my family in church on Christmas Eve, three rows behind a certain boy in my youth group. I had sung in the junior youth choir several years ago for the Christmas service, and had also been a candle lighter in other years. This year I watched my Sunday school teacher's wife, Helen, take the part of the main character in Truman Capote's "A Christmas Memory." As my attention wandered I scanned the audience. When that certain young man came into my sight, I realized that someday I would like to return to the Christmas Eve service and be married to that boy sitting in front of me. Ten years later, on Christmas Eve in 1979, that boy and I dedicated our three-month-old son, Peter, in the same church. We recited "Each night a child is born is a holy night. . . ." Every time I hear that poem by Sophia Lyons Fahs now, I get goose bumps. Like myself, many lifelong UUs have powerful memories of holidays and ceremonies. Because of memories like this one, I started a family Christmas Eve service at the first church where I was a director of religious education. Over the course of my fifteen-year tenure there, this service grew from one experimental lay-led 5:00 pm meeting to two overflowing services. In developing similar initiatives, we hope to create memories that will follow other UUs throughout their lives. The Reverend Jaco B. ten Hove found his early experiences in church empowering as well:

> What I remember most are the all-church events, like pic-nics, Easter Egg hunts, and rummage sales. In fact, I recall as a young adolescent really enjoying being put in charge of the Tool Table at a rummage sale.

Dr. Maria Harris introduces a new understanding of "curriculum" in her book *Fashion Me A People*. She describes the curriculum not only as the notebook of lesson plans or the resources in the library but rather as the "whole church." The curriculum is the potlucks, the sermons, the Sunday school, and the building. With this concept in mind and noting the frequency with which special holiday events were remembered in the lives of lifelong UUs in our survey, consider "ritualizing" local holiday events and celebratory activities like holiday pageants, church fairs, egg hunts, plays, parties, pancake breakfasts, and social action events, as noted on the next page.

Positive Church Memories Up to Age Six

Church School	17
A Sense of Belonging and Friends	10
Youth Choir/Singing	9
Christmas Pageant/Fair/Tree	6
Easter Egg Hunts/Flowers	5

Positive Church Memories From Ages Seven to Twelve

Church School	18
A Sense of Belonging and Friends	16
Family Camp/Overnights/Summer Camp	13
Christmas Pageant/Fair	12
Children's Choir/Singing	10
Parent Involvement	8
Parties	6
Bible Stories	6
Church Across the Street	5
Youth Worship	5
Pancake Breakfasts/Church Suppers	5
Science and Nature Activities	5
Exploring the Building	5
Egypt/Mummies	4
Plays	4
Food Drive/Social Action	4

Because so much depends on local opportunities, rituals, and heritage, few of these activities could be written up as elements of a specific curriculum to be followed in all congregations. A congregation without a building of its own may not be able to put up a Christmas tree, and a congregation without outdoor space may not be able to offer a maypole dance. A strongly humanist congregation may prefer not to sponsor a pagan Samhain service. An established congregation may have long traditions that would compete with the more recently introduced Bridging Ceremony. Congregations with Hispanic heritages might offer a Posadas night at Christmas, while others might sponsor a Kwanzaa or Santa Lucia service.

But within each congregation there is the possibility for creating a "local" curriculum. What is most important in this context aren't the specific rituals themselves, but the idea that yearly congregational traditions need to be explicit and not added as an afterthought at the last moment. This local curriculum should be included in the congregational calendar and planned over the course of the year as carefully as church school lessons are planned. In this way we recognize the value of spiraling through the years and honoring the traditions that make up a congregation's life.

Without proper planning, our local heritages and traditions can be swallowed up by a liberal desire for change for the sake of change. There is a joke among UUs that anything offered more than twice is a tradition that "has always been done." Certainly, this is not the case everywhere. Although UU congregations can become as fossilized as any religious community, we often resist creating a pattern of celebration and ceremony and instead wrack our brains to invent something new each year. Religious educators have been characterized as "agents of radical transformation," and in some congregations so much is being developed and changed that we forget to savor traditions. It is necessary to work towards a balance between stabilty and change in order to create lifelong memories and commitment. Traditional celebrations lend themselves to creating memories that last. Consider former UUA president William F. Schulz's memory of an Easter tradition:

> I grew up in the First Unitarian Church of Pittsburgh and two images in particular of my early childhood in that church remain. One is of its mustiness, a kind of welcoming mustiness, which was never offensive but which has spoken to me ever since (whenever I encounter it) of sweet warmth and history. And the second memory is of Irving Murray's bald spot surrounded protectively by curly hair. Irving Murray was the minister of the church. He was distributing daffodils to the children one Easter and I waited expectantly to hear my name. I was perhaps six. And when by some oversight it never came, I'm sure my eyes welled up with tears. But then—Hosanna!—three pitiful little daffodils remained at the end and Irving, ever quick, asked that any child who had not yet received a gift come forward to make

the claim. Suddenly the skies cleared as I ran to the altar and Irving bent to pick up the flower and in his bending revealed a bald spot set sheepishly amid curly hair. Do you understand how much self-control it took for me not to rub it? For at that moment I had learned that the church was the place that never forgets you and Irving's bald spot somehow was a reflection of its care and memory. I come to this service each year to retrieve for just a moment mustiness, daffodils, and bald spots amid curly hair.

In addition to holidays there are other important celebratory events that need to be shared and named by the congregation. UUs may participate in a variety of rituals marking life-transitions and journeys, such as weddings, services of union, child dedications, and memorials. (My father, Del Tweedie, once remarked that no one would really understand our faith until they experience a UU memorial service.) These rituals reinforce our faith and our commitment to the community. But too often we confine these events to a few participants and neglect to invite the congregation as a whole to take part.

For example, a young man who grew up in a UU church asked to meet with the minister. "I know that UUs believe in freedom and tolerance and all," he said, "but do UUs ever do weddings?" He was thinking of getting married and didn't know if UUs could perform wedding ceremonies. He had actually grown up in the church and had never experienced these important events! This conversation demonstrates that we need to include more about the life of the community in religious education curricula. This too is part of the "local" curriculum.

By listening to lifelong UUs we can learn about the ceremonies and rituals that form a common thread in the lives of our members. There is value in repeating the same candle-lighting ritual in the Christmas Eve service year after year or using daffodils in the Easter service. Each six-year-old who later returns as a fourteen-year-old and still later as a twenty-one-year-old will savor these memories and gain new insights. We need to offer our children ways to understand the services that mark life's journeys and to share with them the importance of including each person's unique gifts in weddings, dedications, and memorial services. Children want and need to repeat experiences. Consider the number of times a child will listen to a favorite song or bedtime story or watch a favorite video. To make memories we need to tell our stories over and over again through celebrations and ceremonies. Part of creating lifelong commitment is knowing and transmitting these stories.

5

Prepare All for the Negative
Side of Community

ONCE WE EMBRACE our UU identity, we begin to recognize the less
desirable aspects of our faith. Perhaps due to an inability to state our
beliefs explicitly, perhaps as a consequence of our liberal idealism,
which can make it hard to accept mistakes and imperfections, we
rarely teach about the downside of our faith community. But part of
learning who we are is recognizing our failings as individuals and as
a community. Like our brothers and sisters in other faith traditions,
we have our squabbles, our problems, and our shortcomings.

UUs can with some justification be accused of elitism and exces-
sive individualism. Lynn Hawley Bootes talks about the negative
consequences of immersion in an environment that can tend to
emphasize the intellectual at the expense of other human elements:

I became rather sensitive to a kind of intellectual elitism that UUs practice. This attitude didn't sit well with me when I had to learn to deal with the emotions of people in all walks of life as a doctor.

And Priscilla Osgood notes a tendency to see our faith as an individualistic pursuit at the expense of the communal:

> After I went off to college and then married, I stopped going to church, first, because there were no UU churches nearby, and later because I was a single mother with three kids, a full time job, and school at night and because I just didn't "need something else to get up and do." In retrospect, I wish I had had a Unitarian Church nearby—it would have been a great support for me *and* my children. But I hadn't ever thought of church in that light.

Responses to the survey indicate an awareness of Unitarian Universalism's flaws from earliest memories into adulthood. But lifers also describe an attempt to cover up problems. Lois Fahs Timmons, daughter of UU religious educator Sophia Lyons Fahs, shares this insight into her experience with religious education in UU congregations. She is quoted in a 2002 *UU World* article about evil:

> We spent ninety-five percent of our time studying good people doing good things, and skipped very lightly over the bad parts of humanity. I was taught not to be judgmental, not to

observe or report on the bad behavior of others. Consequently, because of my education, I grew up ignorant about bad human behavior, incompetent at observing it in others, unskilled in how to respond to it, and ashamed of talking about evil.

In a similar vein, lifelong UU Sharon Hwang Colligan describes what she learned from African-Americans in her book *Children of a Different Tribe*:

> As a UU child, I wasn't taught that there are powerful active organizations in this country that would like to see me and my kind destroyed. Being called a "heretic" and burned at the stake was something that happened only in the distant and foggy past. In college, as I struggled with the culture shock of entering the outside world, I saw that black students had been better prepared than I had been. They knew that the outside world would be full of hostile forces, forces that denied the inherent worth of all people. I had not been told. I was not prepared.

Among their earliest negative memories, survey respondents mention being ostracized by Christian friends, snobbish classmates, and a sense of the church as small, dingy, and far from home. One respondent even mentions the boredom of waiting for parents to finish talking at coffee hour. I tell the children in my fellowship that

I remember rolling my eyes and begging, "Please can we go home now?" We can notice when this happens in our congregations and help children realize that these long conversations are good signs that the family is part of a religious community.

In the elementary school ages, from seven to twelve years old, respondents recall being "forced" to attend services, waiting for adults to finish up at coffee hour, not having other children to play with, being laughed at, and having an awareness of controversies within the program.

In the early teen years—between thirteen and fifteen years old—respondents recall negative memories about sexuality or liberal religious youth, boring adult services, negative memories of subject matter, and church controversies.

Children and teens are clearly aware of the tensions that come with being part of a a community. Given this reality, we should make these tensions explicit and be forthright about our shortcomings. We aspire to our Purposes and Principles, but don't always live up to them. Further, UUs have no ceremonies of confession or atonement as do Catholics and Jews. We need ceremonies of reconciliation and remorse when mistakes are made or when, intentionally or unintentionally, we cause bad things to happen.

When I was growing up we occasionally watched the stop-motion animation show "Davey and Goliath" in the early Sunday hours before my family left for church. Davey was faced with the negative side of life—stealing, fighting, fear—and the show (created by the Lutheran Church) gently explored the consequences and difficulties of doing what was right. I was craving to learn more about the problems I'd face, and I don't think I was the only UU kid who felt this way.

Through our liberal idealism we desire progress, believe in the possibility of good, and value dignity, justice, and freedom. These are good ambitions, but we often neglect to prepare our children and youth for the inevitable suffering and evil they will experience in their lives. Howard Welsh, a UU Vietnam veteran, describes his lack of preparation for the horrors of war. He felt his church had let him down by focusing only on its ideals:

> Our children suffer terribly because of their idealism when they find out what really goes on in the world. Just as I felt when I was drafted into the U.S. military during the Viet Nam War, they feel unprepared and in a sense betrayed. They see the UU faith as being irrelevant to their struggles in a cruel society.

In a personal interview, Welsh underlined the importance of helping children and teens face "the walls" in our society. What will they do when their idealism comes face-to-face with war, injustice, poverty, and other intractable social problems? These realities exist and we need to be prepared for them.

As our lifers became adults, they encountered incidences of betrayal by the community or minister in times of family crisis, ministerial conflict, and congregational disagreement. No congregation is perfect. A congregation may ignore a troubled couple, members might indulge in spiteful gossip, leadership may be politically inept, and confidences can be broken. Betrayals also occur around theological convictions. We can betray our values of inclusiveness and diversity by subtle sneering. Humanists can feel excluded as can our UU Christian brothers and sisters when adult members drift into theological cliques. The Reverend Jaco B. ten Hove illustrates the challenge this way in his church newsletter:

> I've never been a Christian. I say this without pride or contrariness; it's just a fact. I was raised in a good Unitarian congregation that was predominantly Humanist, and I learned a few things about Christianity along the way, but it never attracted me enough that I wanted to "follow" Jesus, especially as he is portrayed by modern Christian churches.... I started running into Unitarian Universalist Christians, and discovered how following Jesus can be a powerful pursuit for liberal religionists. I now count as friends many who are associated with the UU Christian Fellowship, a continental group that sponsors the growth of a kind of Christianity that, to my view anyway, approximates the religion of Jesus in ways I find inspiring, even from a distance. My point is this: I love the fact that there's fruitful room in Unitarian Universalism for Christians, and I'm unhappy that they too

often feel disrespected by arrogant, even narrow-minded non-Christians. If you are inclined to lump all followers of Jesus into a single stereotyped group, I challenge you to think again. . . . And if you would call yourself a Christian UU, I thank you for your courage in moderating what is fast becoming an extremist climate in America.

Jaco ten Hove demonstrates the necessity of naming narrow-mindedness. Better that we name it and learn from it than deny our imperfections—because at some point, to our surprise and dismay, we will find out that UU congregations are human. Deepening our faith involves understanding conflict and betrayal as inevitable human experiences and preparing ourselves for them. If we are lucky, we gain wisdom, humility, and compassion from these experiences. As one participant in the survey wrote: "Lots of strange things happen in churches and elsewhere. Sometimes we learn from them."

Despite these betrayals, lifers remain in our faith. They are like old-growth trees that have weathered many storms and while they know that Unitarian Universalism is imperfect, they still subscribe to the aspirations and hopes that we hold dear, and they know that the faith is wider and deeper than their personal experience.

6

Provide Background for Teachers
in Every Weekly Session Plan

LIFERS PARTICIPATING in this survey noted in their interviews that they often provide history and a broad perspective on Unitarian Universalism for their congregations. They are often knowledgeable about denominational structures, events, and issues, and thus increase the congregation's pool of experiences. Those who possess this kind of experience should be available every time we teach about UU history, heritage, or identity. The Reverend Samuel (Chip) Wright III highlights the need to involve lifers in this process when he states,

> If Unitarian Universalism is to continue to offer what its core values are, it needs navigators to help set the course. Ones

who know the waters bone-deep, not just good chart-readers. Otherwise this grand experiment might well run aground and never again set sail before the wind, which I believe is its true nature.

One of the difficulties in teaching about UU heritage is that there are not enough knowledgeable UUs to tell stories from their own experiences. Often, volunteer teachers in a church school program are new to Unitarian Universalism. And lifers themselves often seek a deeper understanding of what it means to be a UU. Ross Huelster found his UU church's emphasis on inclusivity to be detrimental to his need to define what it meant to be a UU:

> I wondered why we spent so much time in Sunday school learning about world religions. Why didn't we spend more time on Unitarianism?

It is important that we teach those who are teaching our children and include enough background in each curriculum to help adults grasp the issues and understand the context of what they are teaching. Adult teachers remark on the insights they gain from curricula that include thorough background information.

For instance, teachers who are talking with their classes about United Nations Sunday, a common October topic in several curricula, would benefit from a resource that compares the charter of the United Nations with the Principles and Purposes of Unitarian

Universalism. Surprising parallels between the documents might escape a child's awareness but enhance an adult's understanding of the relationship. Additional background might highlight the role of UU statesman Adlai Stevenson as U.S. ambassador to the new United Nations. In addition, it might help teachers to know that the biblical reference from Isaiah to "beating swords into ploughshares" was the basis for the famous Soviet statue that stands outside the UN building.

Sharon Hwang Colligan describes a hunger for depth in Unitarian Universalism that can be met in part by incorporating these broader resources:

> UU young adults ask me: Is Unitarian Universalism strong enough to challenge me? Deep enough to deepen me? Real enough for me to be proud of? Fellowship and comfort are good things, but I can get that at a café. I want to know about the religion. And I want to *feel* its power, not just believe in some principles on paper.

We need to include teacher background for weekly session plans in order to offer depth and honor our commitment to lifelong searching for both the lifelong UUs who are becoming re-involved as adults and for new UUs who are often recruited to teach about a faith that they are just beginning to understand themselves.

7

Provide Parent Handouts
in Every Session Plan

THERE IS A SIGNIFICANT discrepancy in UU religious education between parental expectations and program realities. Parents bring their children to "get some liberal religion," but religious educators know that even if a child comes each Sunday, that still only adds up to about forty hours a year. So religious educators must assume that church school supports what goes on in the home. Yet parents respond, "We don't know what to say!" or "I ask my children what they talked about in class and they answer, 'Oh, nothing.'"

Lifelong UUs often describe a family heritage that models and teaches Unitarian Universalism at home. The families of those who participated in the survey attended Sunday services on an average of three to four Sundays per month, so that a strong UU identity was often part of their family culture. Reverend Margaret Gooding writes about her Universalist home in the 1930s:

> The same climate of reasoning and questioning prevailed in my home and added to it was the pride communicated by my grandparents and my father in belonging to the "no hell" church. There were some fairly strict family rules. But there was always the attitude that "the life you live is up to you, you are responsible for it and you may choose what it will be." No one preached, "Take care of your fellow human beings," but all the grownups—grandma, grandpa, my father, my stepmother, Auntie Etta—did this. The model was there. We did not communicate our feelings to each other very well, and that I regret, but at that time few New Englanders recognized the importance of that at home, church, or school. I guess it all came out at town meetings!

We need to recognize the value of a strong home environment that models UU values. We need to support a home-church connection that explicitly allows for discussion and the integration of the ideas presented in church school. One way of doing this that is often neglected is to provide parent handouts that go home after every weekly session. This technique is commonly used in other denominations that have recognized the importance of providing materials to encourage dialogue at home. We can do the same. We can help our families deepen their Unitarian Universalist faith together.

Few of our published curricula include a prewritten parent handout. My belief in the importance of fostering a home-church connection led me to include a parent handout in my *Chalice Children* curriculum. The UC/UUA's *Our Whole Lives* children's curricula include a "Homelink" for parents. One practical way to help teachers to create a parent handout is to use a generic form that instructors can customize. Visitors will get an idea of the kinds of lessons being offered, and parents will know what kinds of things to ask about that will elicit a response. The handout can be very simple, listing at the top the date, the title of the lesson, the teacher's name, and the teacher's phone number in case parents have questions. The form should include two statements for the student to complete and show to their parents: "Today we . . . ." and "Ask me about. . . ."

8

Offer Opportunities for All Ages
to Live Out UU Values

WHILE SURVEY PARTICIPANTS made only infrequent references to specific social justice experiences, the impact of taking action on the basis of one's values shines through in their personal stories. One respondent recalled, "A speaker from the community made a huge impression on me in terms of social responsibility." Two mentioned service projects. Positive memories from the period between the ages of sixteen and eighteen included the 1968 March on Washington and meeting Martin Luther King Jr. We need to continue to offer opportunities for individuals to *act* based on what they *believe* and for children and adults to work side by side on behalf of these values.

The survey indicates that a high degree of involvement in service projects through UU youth groups and Sunday school was important to respondents, and includes powerful individual testimony to the value of engaging children, teens, young adults, and families in action on behalf of values. The Reverend William F. Schulz reminisces about his conflicting emotions when it came to taking a controversial political stand with the support of his church community:

> I grew up in the First Unitarian Church of Pittsburgh. From the outside that church is a dark, Edwardian disaster. Perhaps in an effort to excuse its architecture, the congregation has periodically painted the sanctuary a different color. It was one color when, as a child, I first attended services with one hand held tightly by each of my parents. And it was another color when, as a young teenager, I participated in my first anti-war vigil there.
>
> And perhaps it had been painted once again when we held in it, in 1974, a memorial service for my mother. But a year ago when I conducted a memorial service in that space for my father, I looked out at that sanctuary before I rose to speak and realized that for me it represents all human continuity. I ignored its present color and thought instead of a youngster's trust, a teenager's fears, and two parents who blessed me beyond description with their devotion.

The Reverend Margaret Gooding's daughter, Fran Tilgner, "an idealist, a student campaigner for Eugene McCarthy, and a protester against the Vietnam War," wrote the following poem after a church service in which she and other college-aged young adults expressed their thoughts and feelings about the Vietnam War. She dedicated the poem to the people of the First Unitarian Universalist Church of Phoenix, Arizona.

Oneness

I'm beginning to learn a oneness, a sameness,
That we aren't really alone or outnumbered.
That there are others who know and care,
Who cry out as we do.
Others—older—different—"straighter" than we.
And maybe their pain is greater, their despair deeper.
After all, they *have* seen more, lived more, hoped and
    dreamed more than we.
They fought the war to end all wars.
And before I was even born conceived the United Nations.
Why should I be so arrogant as to assume that only the
    young have eyes that really see!
That only my generation has dreams of peace and
    brotherhood?
After all, we learned those dreams from the ones we blame!
Why must we assume they have forgotten those hopes—or
    never had them?
Perhaps if my generation could remember who gave us
    those dreams,

And if those teachers could remember what they've taught us,
Perhaps we could all grow together a little, and learn from
each other, and listen.
And maybe—just maybe—build those dreams and find a
oneness too.

The power of community is evident in James T. McCollum's childhood experience of living out UU values even when it meant ostracism:

My family and I became involved in the Unitarian Church in Champaign-Urbana, Illinois, during a very difficult period of time for us, occasioned by a very unpopular lawsuit being prosecuted by my mother, which challenged a program of sectarian religious instruction in the public schools. The case was ultimately decided in our favor by the U.S. Supreme Court in a landmark decision written by Justice Hugo Black. However, the importance of the case and the principle upon which it was grounded escaped the ken of the local gentry. My family and I were outcasts in the community, virtual pariahs, if you will. The Unitarian Church and its minister, the Reverend Phil Schug, offered a port in the storm—the only place where we found acceptance, in what was then a Bible-thumping community. Theologically, we were Humanists and fit right in with the congregation. I was, consequently, raised in that church's Sunday school.

One final piece of testimony is well worth sharing. Joyce Dowling's story highlights the importance of knowing that there are communities of like-minded people who support you as you speak out against things that are unjust.

My favorite story is one I tell when someone asks the question, "How can we tell if our religious education program is doing any good?" My daughter, Maia, started religious education at age three and attended almost every class until age sixteen. In public high school, she was in an assembly where a minister was asked to speak about something in relation to education, but instead he started preaching about the Bible. The principal wasn't present but many teachers were there—and no one said anything. Finally Maia, who is generally shy, stood up and asked, "Haven't you ever heard of 'separation of church and state?'" Later, teachers and students went up to her and told her that she did the right thing. So why couldn't they? I believe it's because they didn't feel the support for these convictions that Maia felt. She had her whole church and denomination behind her. She knew she was doing the right thing with no doubt in her mind. It was definitely her experience in UU religious education that did it for her.

9

Offer Engaging Church School
for Kindergarten through Sixth Grade

THE TIME AND ENERGY required to create, maintain, and grow a religious education program is well spent. The common threads in the memories of lifelong UUs affirm that church school is a powerful way to create a sense of community that will last a lifetime. Seventeen survey respondents noted positive recollections of church school from the period before age six, and eighteen felt the same way about ages seven through twelve; many others identified corollary experiences such as "a sense of belonging and friends" and "singing in youth choir" as positive. Lifers expanded on these pleasant memories of their activities. The Reverend Margaret Gooding recalls:

I went to Sunday school regularly. I learned a lot about the Bible but always with attention to what might have been a reasonable explanation of various phenomena. I particularly remember being told, "Of course the Hebrews had a taboo against pork. It would have been contaminated with trichinosis." Questioning was part of the process too. We questioned the miracles of Jesus; we questioned a whale actually being able to swallow Jonah; we questioned what really kept the lions from eating Daniel. And I remember vividly the Ten Commandments and a question I asked that received no answer. "What is adultery?" "You'd better go home and ask your grandmother," was the only answer the teacher could get out. There were limits in keeping with the cultural taboos of rural New England! I also learned a lot completely unrelated to the Bible. There was no "decision making" course in those days, but I remember well a slim green book called *Everyday Problems*, which elicited much discussion on how to live a good, responsible, and caring life. We were recognized as individuals. We dropped pennies, one each for every year of our ages, in a plaster cake with real candles when we had birthdays. We filled little cardboard baseballs and socks with dimes to help support the Clara Barton and Elliot Joslin Camps for diabetic children run by the Universalist Women's Societies. We spoke pieces on Children's Sunday and had Christmas parties and Sunday school picnics, hikes, and skating parties.

Likewise, Nanette McFadden-Toews has extensive recollections of positive experiences associated with church school:

My first memories of growing up UU are of playing in a tub of soapy water, washing toy dishes in Sunday school. I loved my teacher, Mrs. Burrows, because she let me play in a way that was not permitted at home. I might add that, while I have since lost my enthusiasm for dish washing, I do let my boys play in the suds. In 1967 the new church was completed. In that great room with the upswept roof, my baby brother was dedicated; I played, terrified, at several piano recitals; we decorated Christmas trees; my husband and I were married; and my oldest son participated in his first pageant ("non-speaking sheep no. 5") in Christmas 1997.

Growing up, my brother and I were the ones who pushed my parents out of bed on Sunday morning. For my brother, I believe it was the opportunity to bond with some wonderful mentoring Sunday school teachers. One gentleman, a diabetic, showed the kids how to squirt colored water into insulin bottles to string up for Christmas decorations. Twenty-five years later, we still put them up.

I would start each visit by putting my quarter in the school collection box. The box was designed in such a way that you could choose where you wanted your money to go. I always sent my quarters to "the children of Bangladesh."

As I recall, giving money for the roof of the church was never very popular.

Central to my church experience were the crafts. I always adored doing things with my hands. I remember the ironed straw stars, the clay chalices, and the venerable god's eyes. It was also at Sunday school that I was challenged to expand my rather static definition of art. Mrs. Hulley showed me how to take colored sand and create an image on the floor. We would admire it for a while before it was swept away. From that I learned that a creative act could be temporal.

For Jonathan Angel, the projects assigned in church school were memorable:

Early church school was positive. I even have vague memories of nursery school. I loved the old Martin and Judy stories and remember in particular one about the death of a grandparent. I remember planting seeds and watching them grow . . . being asked to wonder how many stars were in the sky, how many grains of sand were on the beach—my first brush with awe and infinity. And I remember my mother leading worship for the church school and singing that hymn "Dark brown flows the river. . . it flows along forever with trees on either hand."

For some lifers, like Lynn Hawley Bootes, it was special teachers who created the most striking memories while they served as examples:

> My second-grade Sunday school teacher, Rowena Harrison, became a very important person in my life. Later, her death made me think about how I'd like to be like her.

The kind of engaging Sunday school remembered by lifers is created by skilled, caring teachers and programs that balance fun, which keeps children coming back, and teachable moments, which create mature religious individuals. Many curricula already incorporate this balance, but it is important that teachers are aware of the balance and committed to creating it. For a typical session, define one insight or goal to build the class around. For example, for Palm Sunday the insight might be that Jesus went into the desert city of Jerusalem to be met as a teacher, not as a military leader, as some people had hoped. First, teachers can engage the children's interest by asking them to name what they already know about that insight. During a sharing circle, teachers can ask a focusing story such as, "Has anyone ever been to a desert? What was it like?" followed by the traditional biblical story of Jesus' entry into Jerusalem, the Last Supper, and the other events of Easter week. Children can be encouraged to discuss the story and its implications. We can explicitly welcome their questions, for inquiry is one of the practices we value in our UU community. Finally, the lesson can be reinforced with the fun of sensory experiences. A visit from a real donkey will emphasize Jesus' decision to ride a humble beast to show his followers that he was a teacher, not a general. Giving each child a palm front to take home will emphasize that the story took place in a desert. Re-enactment of Jesus' entry into Jerusalem will make the story more memorable. The use of a variety of sensory experiences will appeal to the variety of learning styles in the group. Conclude with a way for the children to integrate the story into their lives. It may be as simple as a question like, "What will you say when someone asks you about Jesus?" or it may ultimately be as complex as a family decision to visit Israel.

10

Take Every Opportunity for Ministers and Lay Leaders to Mentor Children and Teens

IN HIS BOOK *Some Things Remembered*, the Reverend Clinton Lee Scott shares some wry humor about his work as junior minister in a Los Angeles Universalist church in 1923:

> My work and joy were especially with the young people, a lively, responsive group. Hikes in the mountains, outings at the beaches, dramatic productions, and dinners at the church were some of their activities in addition to mid-week evening meetings. They planned an Easter sunrise service in Farnsworth Park somewhere north of Altadena. An hour before dawn our line of cars was moving too fast through Pasadena's deserted streets when two of the boys who were

driving were stopped by an officer of the law and given a summons to appear in court the following day. I represented them at the bar of justice and made an impassioned plea for clemency. They were fined forty-five dollars each, and given forty-five hours in jail for driving forty-five miles an hour in a twenty-five mile speed zone. The question was never settled whether if I had not played advocate they would have fared worse or better.

A group of boys, ages nine to thirteen, were Wigwam Braves. Once on a week's hike in the Sierra Madre Mountains we were all deputized by rangers to fight a raging forest fire. I was fearful for the safety of the boys but they thought the experience a lark. Names and addresses were taken down, and a few days later each Brave received a check and a letter from a forestry official expressing gratitude for services rendered. The remuneration was more than enough to pay the expenses of the outing. Afterward, whenever a forest fire was reported the Braves begged for a hike to the scene of action.

Is ministerial involvement in youth affairs a thing of the past? Do we allot time in a minister's schedule for youth events? It is the rare minister who can find time to visit youth at a YRUU Sunday evening meeting much less attend an overnight or conference. Yet, over and over, lifer participants shared specific instances when a minister or church leader inspired them. "He's the reason I'm in seminary now." "She made a nice compliment to me when I was in junior high that I'll always remember." For the Reverend Suzelle Lynch, direct contact with a particular minister started her on her own path to the ministry:

> Occasionally we attended the "adult service" when there were guest speakers, especially ministerial speakers, and I had my first thought of becoming a minister when I heard the Reverend Denise Tracey speak.

Likewise, Eugene Navias describes the effect that people who took to the time to minister to youth had on his own UU development:

> It was at Rowe Camp that Bob Killiam, the minister of my church in Cleveland, Ohio, and director of the camp, invited me along with others to conduct the evening chapel services and coached us in selecting and designing our speeches and in speaking effectively. The best public speaking lessons I ever had were from him and I gained a sense that I had some capacity for creating and leading worship. It was at Rowe that I met Angus MacLean, John Murray Atwood, and Max Kapp, three of the four members of the faculty of the Theological School at St. Lawrence. It was also at Rowe that Bob Killiam took a special interest in me and started talking to me about ministry.

If we hope to make our young people's faith a lifelong commitment, then we must make sure that our leaders have time to notice and appreciate our youth. Our society often treats youth as anonymous. Yet the responses of lifelong UUs bear witness to the power of having one's emerging talents recognized.

Another common thread for lifers is recalling fond memories of working with adults in a leadership capacity between the ages of thirteen and fifteen. This type of mentoring was listed twenty-three times, second only to youth group memories (twenty-six). As the Reverend Albert C. Niles explains, positive youth group experiences balanced with opportunities for mentoring from leaders in the congregation are a powerful mixture:

> My father had been chaplain of the Colorado House of Representatives for a couple of terms. Following that he became chaplain of the State Senate. Now and then I would accompany him when the legislature was in session and got to meet such people as the governor, Ed Johnson, who eventually became a U.S. Senator. Some years later, in the mid-1920s to 1930s, when the Universalist Church of America held its General Convention in Washington, D.C., both my parents and I were in attendance. When Senator Johnson learned of this, he told his secretary he would be unavailable for the afternoon and he took us on a personal tour of our nation's capital.

Leadership opportunities during teen years that are remembered and noted in response to the survey are:

- assisting or teaching in Sunday school
- speaking in church
- counting ballots at the congregational meeting
- participating in the adult theatre group
- leading worship
- meeting guest speakers
- leading worship for Sunday school
- helping with a lecture series.

In closing, we might ask ourselves the following questions. What kinds of leadership and mentoring opportunities are you providing for your young people? How are your ministers and lay leaders noticing and spending time with your teens?

11

Sweep Teens into Immersion Experiences

REVEREND EUGENE NAVIAS, former director of religious education for the Unitarian Universalist Association and one of our most beloved leaders and ministers, describes his immersion experience at Rowe Camp in Western Massachusetts:

Rowe was the carrot *par excellence*, a Unitarian youth camp. The whole church, even the Ladies Alliance, was behind your going, and they gave enough money so that everyone in the group went whether or not their parents could afford it. Rowe Camp meant Bob Killiam, the director; Jimmy Newlands and Priscilla Leighton, counselors; and a lot of wonderful people who clearly influenced the course of my life. Bob believed that there was nothing more important in his ministry than his work with young people; all through his ministry, he found significant ways of being engaged with them. It was at Rowe that I found a corner of Unitarianism Universalism that suited both my mind and my heart, where I found worship that fed my spiritual hungers. In those years, I graduated from the religion of my parents to a religion of my own. I perceived that my home church was overly "research rational" and I hungered for something more. At Rowe, I found it. I could now claim Unitarianism Universalism for myself."

Ross Huelter also remembers UU summer camp very fondly:

I attended a summer camp sponsored by the Willmar, Minnesota Unitarian Church one week a summer for ten or eleven years. The core group of campers remain near, dear friends, even if we're in touch infrequently. I grew up with these kids in many senses of the word.

For many lifers, immersion experiences provide some of the most significant memories of their UU youth. In the survey, attending camps and conferences is the second most frequently mentioned positive experience for lifelong Unitarian Universalists. In fact, twenty-six lifers recollect positive experiences being part of a youth group between both ages thirteen and fifteen and between ages sixteen and eighteen. These numbers suggest how very important this aspect of our curricula is.

Immersion experiences include retreats, conferences, camps, and special trips. While it does take a good deal of effort to provide teens with the emotional "highs" that they seek, the experiences of talking to a friend all night, worshipping together, watching the stars, dancing freely, being a leader, finding a mentor, and retreating from everyday life into "sacred space" create lifelong memories and indelible impressions. For some, like the Reverend Jaco B. ten Hove, summer camp became the springboard for a lifetime in the UU ministry:

> LRY and Homestead Camp [a project founded in 1959 by Community Church in New York City] were full of leadership roles for me. I remember one summer a quartet of us teenage guys saying something like, "Any church that has a camp like this can't be all bad, so let's grow up and become UU ministers." Two of us did many years later.

Immersion experiences also include those weekend conferences that have been extremely important experiences in the lives of lifelong UUs. Sharon Hwang Colligan, a Unitarian Universalist young adult, describes her interviews with young adults about the conference experience, emphasizing the difficulty UUs have in trying to capture the deeply moving experience in words:

> I met with some district YRUU leaders who were aging out

and were interested in talking about creating conferences for UU young adults. "Because," they said, "there is such a deep need."

Their eyes and their body language were full of urgency and yearning and the fear of unbearable loss.

"Yes," I said. "I know. I understand. But, um—just for the record—can you tell me what, specifically, you think is needed? So I can have it in your words. So I can make sure that UU Young Adult Network works to meet it."

"Conferences," their leader said. Her body language put a universe into that one word. But then she stopped.

"But what kinds of things at conferences?" I persisted. "What kinds of activities? What kinds of qualities, what kinds of experiences? What would fill that important need?"

She didn't know how to answer me. I was a fellow UU; I was supposed to just know what the word *conferences* meant. She tried more meaningful glances, more urgent body language, more vivid energy exchanges. I persisted in asking for words.

Someone else tried. "You know. Community." Someone else said, "Workshops." And then, "And uh, you know, worship and stuff." I tried, but that was as far as we ever got. Four words: *conferences, community, workshops, worship.* These were intelligent, beautiful young people trying to communicate to me about experiences that had formed the emotional, spiritual, and social center of their lives—about a community program in which they were considered to be the leadership —and they could not find more than four words to say what it was.

That conversation stayed with me, haunted me. Their urgency, and their inability to speak. "There is such a need," they told me. That part they were able to say. "There is really an urgent need. Such a need for it." But what is "it?"

Colligan goes on to describe a Friday night conference during which the participants are sitting scattered in rows and listening to music but not interacting. Fifteen hours later on Saturday morning, the participants are now...

. . . . sitting close to one another, in groups or piles. Their bodies lean trustingly against one another. Hugs have become part of a normal greeting; reassuring or affectionate touch has become part of a normal conversation. Normal conversation is no longer the polite social chat of the evening before; now it is a free-flowing sharing of the heart, of real-life issues, or a sharing of silliness, of spontaneous word games and free-association humor.... Walking into the conference after a morning errand in the outside world I can feel the conference like a strong energy field that is warm, like a physical warmth; relaxing, like a bubble bath or a day at the beach. It's this energy field that YRUU calls *community*.

A YRUU conference is a religious ritual. I think a closer word for that magical feeling that YRUU calls *community* is actually *communion*. Because it feels like a relaxing bath, I've been calling it "The Magic Pool of Communion." This Magic Pool is a powerful thing—a powerful ritual and a powerful spiritual experience. As far as I can tell, it is the UU conversion experience. Not only youth converts, but also young adults, ministers, and lay leaders will tell you that intellectually, they think that UU ideas are nice, but that they first knew they were really UUs when they attended certain conferences, summer camps, assemblies, or retreats. That's why our adult lay leadership schools last for a week and focus so much on bonding: we know that once someone has been to the Magic Pool, chances are high that he or she will serve this movement for life.

Even if they still can't explain what it is.

These immersion experiences also have a negative side, especially because of the power they hold. This power can be reversed to cause cliques, exclusion, and boundary problems. Anyone involved in the dissolution of Liberal Religious Youth in the 1980s—the result of inappropriate boundaries—knows about this power. Immersion experiences take careful supervision and crafting. It is important for responsible adults, role models, and mentors to help with these conferences and camps.

12

Bolster and Protect Youth Groups

THE MOST STUNNING result from the survey was the number of people who mentioned their youth groups as positive experiences. All of the incarnations of youth groups in the denomination's history were mentioned: YPRU (Young People's Religious Union), AUY (Association of Unitarian Youth), LRY (Liberal Religious Youth), and YRUU (Young Religious UUs). Youth group memories for the years between ages thirteen and eighteen were mentioned about four times more often than any other experience that survey respondents shared. In light of these results, it is painful to think of the neglect that teen youth groups suffer in many of our congregations.

The Reverend Albert C. Niles recalls memories of his youth group in Denver in the 1920s:

The most important event of the weekend occurred at Miss Doble's little bungalow on Saturday nights. As the church gang gathered, the rugs were rolled up and stored out of the way. The player-piano was pressed into action. Powdered wax might be scattered on the wood floors, and dancing would commence. If the tune being played had some good words, we sang. The circulation of the dancing traffic went from the front room towards the kitchen then into a back bedroom. From there a narrow hallway went towards the front of the house past a bathroom and storage closets. This then led into a bedroom off the front room. The dancing always went counterclockwise. Eventually the light hanging from the ceiling in the hallway would get turned off; then the evening really got under way.

The Reverend Margaret Gooding speaks of her experience in the youth group of her Universalist congregation:

As a high schooler I sang in the choir and helped teach the little children, playing the piano for them as they sang, 'Clap, clap your hands for joy . . . ' I belonged to the YPCU—the Young People's Christian Union—a forerunner to LRY with the same programming problems that keep cropping up today!

The Reverend Jaco B. ten Hove also found solace in his Liberal Religious Youth group:

Liberal Religious Youth was a huge crucible of formation for me, along with UU summer camp at Homestead…. I ran away from home early in my senior year in the midst of a minor power struggle with my family and moved into an unfinished basement of the religious education building, where I had a small printing operation that produced the Liberal Religious Youth federation newsletter. I made a deal with the custodians who lived upstairs. I got a job at the town library and was prepared to finish my high school career on my own, but my Dad found me after a few weeks and convinced me to return home. But the church was still my sanctuary.

But is all lost if there isn't a critical mass of young people with whom to create a youth group? Not necessarily. The results for early teen years suggest an important alternative. Survey participants reflecting on their experiences from ages thirteen to fifteen noted events such as helping to count ballots during a congregation meeting, joining the adult theatre group, preparing for confirmation, speaking in church services, helping with candles at the Christmas Eve service, and connecting with adults in general and specific adults who were mentors. One respondent recalls that he first thought of being a minister in these young teen years. These results suggest that young teens, especially, need to connect with adults and have access to leadership opportunities. For some of our congregations without a critical mass of teenagers necessary to sustain a youth group, these results suggest that providing meaningful roles for the young teens in the life of the congregation is a powerful way to build UU identity.

Another difference between the memories of younger and older teen years is the importance of the *About Your Sexuality* (*AYS*) and the *Church Across the Street* programs for younger teens. These programs and their more recent counterparts, *Our Whole Lives* (*OWL*) and *Neighboring Faiths*, should be given priority in middle school and/or junior high programming.

In addition, three respondents mention a negative memory that they were not offered explanations of Unitarian Universalism in their early teen years. These results suggest that incorporating UU identity-specific subject matter for young teens is as important in our faith as identity-forming programming, such as confirmation or bar/bat mitzvah, is in others.

Respondents note increased opportunities to meet notable people in their later teen years as opposed to when they were younger teens. This result suggests the importance of heroes and role models for older teens. In order to create these experiences for teens in your church, bring in prominent speakers (including members of your own congregation) to make lasting memories. Also, organize outings to presentations by notable speakers, activists, and the movers and shakers of contemporary society.

Of course, when they are not given proper supervision and mentoring, youth groups can be a source of negative experiences and painful memories Seven respondents cite youth groups as negative experiences. Being shy, not feeling safe, being left out of cliques, and tension around youth issues are mentioned frequently. In interviews with lifelong UUs, more seriously damaging memories of sexual abuse, inappropriate behavior from advisors, and substance abuse are mentioned as negative memories of teen years in UU youth groups. The teen years are edgy times. A youth group is a place where a highly volatile mix of active, creative, and experimenting teens are exploring boundaries and finding their place in the world, and this can be a dangerous undertaking. A youth group requires balanced, mature, creative, and flexible leadership, governance, and guidelines to protect the youth group experience for our teens. Maintaining a healthy youth group under healthy advisors requires a commitment to provide financial and leadership resources. However, the lasting commitment to our faith that youth groups can impart to young people is worth the investment.

A positive youth group experience may be the most important facet of creating a committed lifelong Unitarian Universalist. Many other religious groups already know this. In the Western United States, it is common to see Mormon bishops accompanying a youth group on a rafting trip. Baptist, Methodist, and Lutheran church buses filled with excited teens show up at Colorado ski towns from all over the country.

The 1996 UUA General Assembly, which focused on youth, initiated a number of positive changes. It has entered our denominational awareness that we can and should encourage youth delegates at GA. I was personally struck by the need to address teens in their own language and to respond to their own cultural mores as I witnessed the introduction of two young teens to the larger denomination during the banner parade at the Cleveland General Assembly. Because Cleveland was the home of the Rock and Roll Hall of Fame, the music for the parade was hopping and jumping. As the two boys passed my row carrying their congregation's banner, I overheard one exclaim, "Wow! They never play music like this at home!" I suspect that they came away from the experience with a new vision of Unitarian Universalism. Jane Clayton makes a similar point discussing her own experiences around 1970:

> I enjoyed our Liberal Religious Youth meetings. It was the "hippie" era. We meditated, read poetry, and met a UU minister named Rick Masten from Big Sur, California, who wrote songs and poems that were perfect for our times. I helped plan and organize a very large LRY conference in Ottawa. It was a very enlightening time in my life.

The youth group experience should help keep youth connected to the congregation and the denomination. Youth groups should help young people to be visible in congregations and take on meaningful responsibilities as they accomplish the transition to adult membership.

13

Connect with Our Young Adults

THERE WERE NOTABLY few responses to the part of the survey that asked UUs to reflect on their experiences between the ages of nineteen and twenty-one, as many of the respondents were not involved in a UU congregation or group in their young adult years. The Reverend Suzelle Lynch writes,

> I was a leader waiting to be asked, and ended up creating my own opportunities in the young adult community out of a need for spiritual worship, quite frankly. But if the church had gotten hold of me before that, I could have poured all that energy and skill into their programs. Raised-up UUs come into our congregations as young adults with "jet packs"

on—they don't need the warm-up those who were not raised UU seem to need.

Lynn Hawley Bootes notes the lack of UU services on her college campus as contributing to her own lack of interest at that time:

It is just very difficult to connect the campus or young adult lifestyle with Sunday church attendance. I would have participated more if services were available on campus.

Respondents' church attendance dropped off dramatically in their young adult years, falling to an average of 1.8 Sundays per month for those who had a connection to a UU community. The sixteen respondents who shared memories of their involvement in Unitarian Universalism between ages nineteen and twenty-one listed the following positive experiences:

Sunday School Teaching	6
Ministry Student	4
Attending Home Church During Holidays	4
Attending College Campus Club	3
Going to UU Church with Other Students	3
Getting Married in a UU Church	3
YPRU/LRY/Youth Group	3
Camps	3

Lifers describe a variety of singular experiences as young-adult UUs, including attending worship with a grandfather, visiting other UU churches around the country, picnics, working at Beacon Press, attending General Assembly, riding to church with college faculty, and being invited to church suppers.

One respondent poignantly recounts how, as a freshman college student, she came down with the flu just before Thanksgiving break and ended up staying in her dorm instead of going home. Homesickness and the echoing emptiness of the deserted dorm added to the misery of having the flu. Somehow the local UU minister found out about her plight and delivered chicken soup and orange juice to her. The respondent was very grateful and always felt that she had been taken care of away from home.

Equally important, however, is the fact that of the sixteen respondents in this category, ten mention the negative experiences of feeling no connection to, or encouragement to be a part of, a UU congregation. These responses underscore the importance of connecting with our young adults in order to create a lifelong faith. In my own life, I connected by chance with other UUs at Kalamazoo College in Michigan. As a freshman, I had formed close friendships among some creative, idealistic people. We never discussed religion until the fall semester of our sophomore year. While dreaming up a Halloween visit to the cemetery, I happened to mention that I was a Unitarian. "What!?" said Zander, one of the leaders of the group. "Yeah, I was in a group called Liberal Religious

Youth," I said, but before I could finish Zander said, "I was President of LRY in Lansing!" Another friend chimed in that he had been involved in LRY too. We had found each other by commonality of spirit and outlook on the world. When I transferred to another college, I longed for other UU connections.

Sharon Hwang Colligan shares the following about the experience of being a UU young adult:

> In my work doing young adult networking and ministry I have met many young ex-YRUUers who still suffer from the loss of their beloved spiritual home in the vibrant and intimate UU youth tribe. The absence of UUA young adult programming created a "cliff" at the end of the high school years, instead of a bridge to a spirited UU young adult experience. The pain of seeing the wounded ex-youth, combined with the hopes generated by the growing UU young adult movement, including the very moving Bridging Ceremony, prompted me to write this fantasy letter from the denomination to the 90 percent of its children who never return home.

> *From the Elders to All the UU Youth Who Fell Off a Cliff*
>
> We're sorry
> for all of you, our beloved UU youth,
> who were pushed from your spiritual home
> just because of a number or an age:
> we're sorry.

For all who tried to walk the Bridge
to young adult community
and found it led to nothingness
or worse, to injury at the hands of other UUs
further along the bridge to nothing:
we're sorry.

For you who search with such skill and energy
in so many other places,
trying and trying to find the home you have lost:
we're sorry.

You deserve better.
You deserve your own natural UU home,
the home you blessed with such powerful magic as a youth,
the home that belongs to you.

It was our mistake to send you away.
We somehow imagined it would make you more free.
In our own lives, most of us left the church of our youth.
We thought that you must want to do the same.
We forgot about the pain.
We're sorry.
We did not mean to stop loving you.
We're working now on building a Bridge.
But we know that for a long time there was no bridge at all,
just a cliff at the end of your childhood

or a bridge that led to something incomplete.

A new young adult should be welcomed with joy
but instead we told you goodbye.
We're sorry.

We do love you.

Some of you survived the abandonment
and went on to shine bright and strong.
From our distance we do watch you proudly.

Some of you fell hard and were hurt.
In your eyes we see your shock, anger, fear,
cynicism, indifference, and loneliness.
From our distance, we do weep in pain.
Some of you tried to build the bridge yourselves,
bravely brick by brick,
with no strong connection from the other side.
We have watched the valiant half-bridge
dwindle and twist, crumbling in its incompleteness,
seen many young travelers stumble and fall,
leap off in disgust,
or even be thrown by protective bridge owners.
From our distance, we kept quiet, telling ourselves
that your loneliness was freedom.

Some of you stubbornly climbed the cliff,
returned to us,

woke us from our trance of shame,
demanded we write this apology,
moved us at last to action.
We do it gladly.

We're sorry we sent you away.
It was a terrible mistake.
We love you. Please come home.
We will make you a warm nest
and a room of your own.

We treasure the gifts that you gave us.
We're sorry we hurt you.
Come home.
Come home.

The UUA Young Adult Office has excellent resources. But we haven't resolved who does the work of guiding and supporting efforts for young adults in local congregations. One hole in which young adult programming languishes is created by the perception that religious education is for children and youth, served by a director, with the parish minister serving adults on the other side. That leaves a gap in staffing for emerging young adults. We have increasingly come to recognize that religious education is a lifelong endeavor, of which young adult programming is an important piece, and that it merits the participation of ministers and trained professionals.

But before we throw up our hands at the difficulty of organizing a campus ministry or a young adult group, how about starting with a simple first step based on the survey responses of lifelong UUs? A holiday homecoming reception for returning college students and working young adults would go a long way toward letting young adults know that they are still a part of their home congregation. It is affirming to ask these alumni to be a part of the service, whether by giving readings, reflecting on the experience of returning, or simply lighting a chalice and sharing in communal joys and concerns.

It is worth staying in touch. Our UU young adults and other young people who are searching for a spiritual home like ours need us. And if we do our part, then they will share in the sense of comfort the Reverend Suzelle Lynch discusses in her chapter of Scott Alexander's book *Salted with Fire*:

> When I first came back to the church, I used to sit in the back row of the sanctuary and cry. I wasn't sure why I was crying, all I knew was that I had an almost overwhelming feeling of "coming home." The church I returned to was very different from the one in which I grew up; for one thing, it was almost ten times as big. But the sentiments being expressed from the pulpit were just the same, and they affirmed the beliefs I held most strongly and confirmed ideas I had held all my life. I knew I had found my place, and I wondered why I'd stayed away for so long.

14

Sing Together

WHAT PLEASURE I TAKE in Psalm 66:1, "Make a joyful noise unto God!" Growing up Unitarian Universalist, I had few experiences of joyful singing and many more experiences of intellectual discourse. Now, after a career of singing with colleagues at religious education conferences, leading worship, attending youth conferences, and other powerful singing events, I love making a joyful noise!

If we want to help make our faith a lifelong commitment, it behooves us to support choirs for children, teens, and adults. Many lifelong UUs mention singing together and participating in church choirs as some of their most notable memories:

Remembered Positive Experiences of Singing and Choir
> 0-6 years old—9
> 7-12 years old—10
> 13-15 years old—5
> 16-18 years old—4

In many UU congregations, music programs are marginalized and understaffed. UU musicians struggle to be recognized as full professionals and must advocate for the importance of music ministry in UU communities. Yet music is something that we desperately need. It provides overly intellectual UUs with a powerful way of connecting with transcendent feelings.

In our social justice work, as Dr. Helen Bishop explained at General Assembly (2002), music can connect us to the ground of our being when all seems lost or threatened, especially when we are engaged in the sometimes frustrating pursuit of social justice. She recounted the despair she shared with thousands of others who were crestfallen and angry when Harvey Milk was assassinated. The song "One More Step" pulled her through and gave her hope once again.

The Reverend Eugene Navias also recounts how music and ministry have intertwined in his life:

> Not having a choir in our Unitarian church and wanting the
> experience of singing in one, I sang in the Baptist choir where
> I learned a lot of religious music and heard a lot of theology
> I didn't believe in. Here the strands of religion and music met.

From childhood on I came to love hymns and the singing of them. I remember the hymns from the old Beacon Hymnal: "The ships glide in at the harbor's mouth." I remember singing them with great verve, and eventually as a teenager being entrusted to play them for others to sing ... and I find my memory leaping to playing hymns for preaching class on the old electric organ at St. Lawrence, to playing hymns on the little reed foot-pedal organ at Star Island, to playing hymns a week ago at the UUA chapel at 25 Beacon Street.

Years ago Holly Hollerorth, the UUA's religious education curriculum editor at the time, asked me to provide a few historical hymns for a project called "The Disagreements That Unite Us." What started with collecting and peering at the tiny print in antique hymnals and psalm books eventually resulted in the publication of *Singing Our History*. Coaxing our congregations into song and seeing their ready response has affirmed again and again my belief that the rational needs the passionate.

15

Celebrate Founders, Lifers and Heritage

IN HER SERMON on the creation of the Purposes and Principles, "A Free and Responsible Search: The Story," the Reverend Francis Manly describes the process by which our covenant was created.

They took it to the General Assembly in Philadelphia in 1981, and the delegates there realized that this was much too big and important to be done quickly, or by a few people. Maybe some of them were thinking politically—that if the revised principles were really going to be accepted, then a whole lot of people needed to be involved in creating them, and of course, that was true. But consciously or unconsciously, I think they also understood that the kind of meaning they were reaching for couldn't come from just a few individuals; it was something that could only be found in the collective wisdom of the whole community of faith.

So they created a committee charged with setting up a great process which would involve thousands of people in congregations all across the continent, over the next two or three years. In churches and fellowships and societies, large and small, groups met to wrestle with questions like: Should we change our Principles? Should we even have any formal Principles? What does it mean to have Principles in our by-laws? What's missing? What doesn't belong? What kind of language would we use? Who is included here? Who is left out? What ideals and values are really important to us? What they were really asking themselves was, what does it mean to be Unitarian Universalist? And even deeper down, what does it mean to be human?

Out to the congregations it went, and back to General Assembly, and out to the congregations for more reflection and discussion, and finally back to General Assembly in Columbus, Ohio, in 1984. Though not everyone realized it at the time, it was one of the great moments in the history of our movement. After all the years of study and work and preparation, there was still arguing and amending and wran-gling, like a congregational meeting a hundred times over— but in the end, there was agreement. And something new was born. Not just a revision of the old statement, but a whole new covenant: a new and solemn promise to ourselves and to each other about what we value most and how we will strive to live.

It was a free and responsible search for truth and meaning on a grand scale. Our whole liberal faith community was struggling together to define those things we hold most important, working together to articulate a statement of meaning in which each of us, in all our diversity, could find a place.

To me, the whole process that produced these Principles is wonderful—literally, I am filled with wonder. Because it worked so well. Because of what came out of it. And above all, because the process itself shows us some of the most important things the Principles are about. Yet this is a part of our Unitarian Universalist story that we hardly ever tell—hardly ever to adults, even more seldom, if ever, to our children. Maybe it's so recent it still feels more like news than history. But it's a story we need to hear.

Manly's sermon is used as a teaching tool to train religious educators on UU identity. It is often the first introduction these leaders have to the background of our Purposes and Principles. We need to emphasize our history and heritage in our teaching if we are to show that our faith is responsive to new understandings; it is not knowledge handed down from on high. Our faith is dynamic, formed in the crucible of people's interactions and shared journeys with one another. Demonstrating how our faith has evolved in response to changing times offers our members a means of understanding that ours is a faith of people in process, making decisions, working toward what they believe in.

In order to transmit our faith, we need to tell stories of those who came before us. We have many stories of our origins, such as the arrival of Universalism in the United States through Thomas Potter and John Murray, and stories of courage, such as Unitarian Dorothea Dix's work on behalf of the mentally disabled. In addition to stories about famous Unitarians and Universalists, we need to be sure that we also savor local founders and visionaries.

In UU congregations housed in historical churches in the center of New England towns, this may already be happening. In the start-up congregation or the twenty-five-year-old congregation where I serve, we are just beginning to tell these stories. In many cases, founders are still a part of the congregation, though they may be elderly and frail. For all congregations, telling stories is a reminder that generations will be a part of the institution. Part of teaching the faith is passing on these stories.

Use this checklist to review the place of history and heritage in your local congregation:

- ☐ Do you have a history of your congregation in writing? Can you name someone who can tell the story?

- [ ] Do you know who keeps the archives? Where are the rosters of early church school attendance?

- [ ] Do you tell the story of the congregation's founding to adult, teen, and children on a regular basis?

- [ ] Is there a founders' day celebration?

- [ ] Have names of founders and significant people in the life of the congregation been included in a historical plaque or commemorative item?

- [ ] Are there photo albums of early congregational events? Recent ones for posterity? Are these albums shown to children, teens, and adults?

- [ ] Is there an endowment fund that can accept gifts to benefit the future?

- [ ] Have you saved the notable artifacts and items that contribute to the telling of the history of the congregation, such as a painting of the original church, an original cornerstone, silver service, or offering plates that can be saved and displayed? Is there a guide to these items?

- [ ] Is there a place where church school "graduates" may sign their names as seniors?

- [ ] Are membership books kept safely? Are dedications and weddings recorded for posterity?

If you checked:

8-10 items—Congratulations, your congregation is truly celebrating and savoring its history and heritage. Now it's time to find (or found!) a new congregation and nurture its sense of history and heritage.

4-7 items—You are on the road to a healthy sense of history and heritage. Try adopting one new item per year to celebrate and savor your congregational identity.

0-3 items—You are in a time warp with no past, only a present. And that means the danger of no future. Research, document, and share your history and heritage and find out how rich your celebrations can become.

Conclusion

LIFELONG UNITARIAN UNIVERSALIST Darcy Hall of South Orange, New Jersey, wasn't very active in any congregation from age twenty-two to thirty, being "madly in love" with a boyfriend (and later husband) who was anti-church. But she reports they are currently very active. Her formerly anti-church husband is now the president of the board. "I guess my UU evangelism finally worked," she says, "As a family we are involved in religious education, social action, church governance, everything."

Lifelong commitment can be an enriching and rewarding experience. We need to help our children and teens experience both our faith and our identity in such a way that they will grow up with a faith they can draw on and contribute to as adults. If we claim our *identity* as a *faith*, we will begin to better understand the strengths and weaknesses of our beliefs and assumptions. Using Rebecca Parker's metaphor, our faith will be like a house. We can remodel our house when we need to, but we need to start from somewhere. We can accept responsibility for our house and become critically self-aware of what it conveys both to those in it and to those walking by.

UUs who grew up in the faith and stayed connected have identified with our message. Through youth group or immersion experiences, through family heritage and involvement, and from experiences in the world, they came to understand the implicit assumptions and to adopt them as their own. We can ask lifers to share their stories and their understanding of our faith. We need to nurture the common threads that helped keep people in our faith so that others will more readily see Unitarian Universalism as a faith worthy of a lifelong commitment.

During a retreat of religious professionals I attended some years ago, we divided into small groups and posed the question, "Is Unitarian Universalism a faith?" Several people maintained that it really wasn't a faith in itself but rather a method of learning about other faiths. I struggled to describe what I felt so deeply—that we are indeed a faith. How could my memories of family weddings, memorials, the joys and challenges of community, tears at services, and moments of transcendence be other than a faith? I was tongue-tied. I had no answer then. But this book is my answer, and the answer of the many lifers who have shared their insights and memories with me. It is a beautiful, thrilling, and difficult journey to see faith through varied life experiences. We do have a theology and an identity —one that can be part of the fabric of a life richly lived. We have our many failings and it is time that we come to terms with them. But the aspirations of our faith—our hope for good, our willingness to learn and change, and our companionship on the journey together—make it a powerful life-enhancing commitment.

Through sharing their enthusiasm, lifers help us grow. Let us savor and enjoy their stories as they spiral through a lifetime of commitment. The Reverend Julie-Ann Silberman-Bunn writes,

> From ages five to thirteen, I had the same Sunday school teacher. I left that church at age thirteen to attend a church with a stronger youth program. Years later, after graduating from theological school, I was hired as the first religious education director that congregation had ever had. The first Sunday when it was announced that I had been hired, my childhood Sunday school teacher shouted from the back of the sanctuary, "She's one of mine!" She was still teaching Sunday school. Later that year, when I was ordained, she lit that congregation's chalice at the service. I felt like I had come full circle.

The Survey

A TOTAL OF 82 lifelong UUs responded to the survey, ranging in age from twenty-five to eighty-seven. Of these, nineteen are ministers and seven are children of ministers. Respondents are from twenty-two states and Canada; twenty-five are men and fifty-seven are women.

The survey is provided on the following pages. You may want to consider distributing this survey to lifelong Unitarian Universalists in your own congregation to see what you can learn from them.

Rate your level of Sunday morning attendance during the following times of your life.

Age range	Level of attendance (1 being less than once a month; 5 being every Sunday and then some!)							Average response
0-6 years	0	1	2	3	4	5	na	4.0
7-12 years	0	1	2	3	4	5	na	4.2
13-15 years	0	1	2	3	4	5	na	3.8
16-18 years	0	1	2	3	4	5	na	3.3
19-21 years	0	1	2	3	4	5	na	1.9
22-30 years	0	1	2	3	4	5	na	2.2
31-50 years	0	1	2	3	4	5	na	4.1
51-70 years	0	1	2	3	4	5	na	4.5
71+ years	0	1	2	3	4	5	na	3.6

Rate the level of church involvement for your family of origin during the following times of your life.

Age range	Level of attendance							Average response
	(1 being little extra church work; 5 being many hours of involvement.)							
0-6 years	O	1	2	3	4	5	na	3.8
7-12 years	O	1	2	3	4	5	na	4.1
13-15 years	O	1	2	3	4	5	na	3.9
16-18 years	O	1	2	3	4	5	na	3.7
19-21 years	O	1	2	3	4	5	na	3.4
22-30 years	O	1	2	3	4	5	na	3.3
31-50 years	O	1	2	3	4	5	na	3.3
51-70 years	O	1	2	3	4	5	na	3.1
71+ years	O	1	2	3	4	5	na	3.1

Name the congregations you attended during the following times of your life.

0-6 years

7-12 years

13-15 years

16-18 years

19-21 years

22-30 years

31-50 years

51-70 years

71+ years

List the positive church-related events that occurred during the following times of your life.

0-6 years

7-12 years

13-15 years

16-18 years

19-21 years

22-30 years

31-50 years

51-70 years

71+ years

List the negative church-related events that occurred during the following times of your life.

0-6 years

7-12 years

13-15 years

16-18 years

19-21 years

22-30 years

31-50 years

51-70 years

71+ years

List the leadership opportunities in your congregation that you participated in during the following times of your life.

0-6 years

7-12 years

13-15 years

16-18 years

19-21 years

22-30 years

31-50 years

51-70 years

71+ years

Are there anecdotes and stories about your lifelong experience with the Unitarian and/or Universalist faith that you would be willing to share with other UUs?

Resources

Alexander, Scott W., ed. *Everyday Spiritual Practice: Simple Pathways for Enriching Your Life*. Boston: Skinner House Books, 1999.

_____, ed. *Salted with Fire: UU Strategies for Sharing Faith and Growing Congregations*. Boston: Skinner House Books, 1994.

Beach, George Kimmich. *Questions for the Religious Journey: Finding Your Own Path*. Boston: Skinner House Books, 2002.

Bossen, Colin, and Dawn Star Borchelt. *The Bridging Program: Workshops and Guidelines*. Boston: Unitarian Universalist Association, 2004.

Bumbaugh, David E. *Unitarian Universalism: A Narrative History*. Chicago: Meadville Lombard, 2000.

Collier, Kenneth W. *Our Seven Principles in Story and Verse: A Collection for Children and Adults*. Boston: Skinner House Books, 1997.

Essex Conversations Coordinating Committee. *Essex Conversations: Visions for Lifespan Religious Education*. Boston: Skinner House Books, 2001.

Heller, Anne Odin. *Churchworks: A Well-Body Book for Congregations*. Boston: Skinner House Books, 1999.

Mendelsohn, Jack. *Being Liberal in an Illiberal Age: Why I Am a Unitarian Universalist*. Boston: Skinner House Books, 1995.

Nieuwejaar, Jeanne Harrison. *The Gift of Faith: Tending the Spiritual Lives of Children*. Boston: Skinner House Books, 2002.

Owen-Towle, Tom. *Growing a Beloved Community: Twelve Hallmarks of a Healthy Congregation*. Boston: Skinner House Books, 2004.

Sinkford, William G., ed. *The Unitarian Universalist Pocket Guide*, 4th Ed. Boston: Skinner House Books, 2004.

Wells, Barbara, and Jaco B. ten Hove. *Articulating Your UU Faith: A Five-Session Course*. Boston: Unitarian Universalist Association, 2003.